The Book Of Paul

The Wit And Wisdom Of Paul Keating

Compiled By Russell Marks

16pt

Read How You Want
LARGE PRINT BOOKS, BRAILLE & DAISY

Copyright Page from the Original Book

Published by Black Inc.,
an imprint of Schwartz Publishing Pty Ltd
37–39 Langridge Street
Collingwood Vic 3066 Australia
email: enquiries@blackincbooks.com
http://www.blackincbooks.com

National Library of Australia Cataloguing-in-Publication entry:

The book of Paul : the wit & wisdom of Paul Keating /

compiled by Russell Marks.

9781863956727 (paperback)

9781922231734 (ebook)

Keating, Paul, 1944---Quotations.

Politicians--Australia--Quotations.

Australian wit and humor.

Marks, Russell, compiler.

320.994

Printed in Australia by Griffin Press. The paper this book is printed on is certified against the Forest Stewardship Council® Standards. Griffin Press holds FSC chain of custody certification SGS-COC-005088. FSC promotes environmentally responsible, socially beneficial and economically viable management of the world's forests.

FSC
www.fsc.org
MIX
Paper from
responsible sources
FSC® C009448

IF TONY ABBOTT ENDS UP THE PRIME MINISTER OF AUSTRALIA, YOU'VE GOT TO SAY, GOD HELP US. [HE IS] TRULY AN INTELLECTUAL NOBODY [AND HAS] NO POLICY AMBITION.

ALEXANDER DOWNER

The idiot son of the aristocracy.

Brother, taking you into Elizabeth Bay House is like dragging a hog into the Sistine Chapel, I can assure you.

He is the Christmas turkey.

Howard has been sending a boy on a man's job for years. [on Downer as foreign minister]

TONY ABBOTT

I don't know who should lead the Liberals, but I mean, I know who I wouldn't be going for.
If they take Tony Abbott, they're just going to go back downhill to wherever they've been.
He's the one most like Howard ideologically – he's what I call the young fogey. Howard was the old fogey. He's the young fogey.

KIM BEAZLEY

What would he know from roaming around the Western Australian branch and visiting Pommies in nursing homes? Look at him, he lost an election and he's still walking around like a big cuddly bear. I told him I see it like the *National Geographic* ad, where in slow motion the wildebeest grabs the lion on the arse, with blood and fur and dust and shit flying everywhere. That's what the mob wants in the last fortnight of a campaign – a sign that you really want it. Kim didn't give that to them last time. He's fucking hopeless.

JOE HOCKEY

KEATING: Silly – what's his name? The "Shrek", whoever he was on the television this morning. What's his name?
TONY JONES: Joe Hockey.
KEATING: Yes, Joe Hockey.

I FANCY MALCOLM IS LIKE THE BIG RED BUNGER.
YOU'RE LIGHTING UP, THERE'S A BIT OF A FIZZ, THEN NOTHING. NOTHING.
[ON MALCOLM TURNBULL]

STEPHEN SMITH

He's always between a shit and a
shiver.

PETER COSTELLO

PETER COSTELLO: Mr Speaker, I rise
on another point of order.
This really is going on for far too long.
As you know, questions have to be
short and to the point so those opposite
can answer them. I suggest that you
instruct the minister to wind up because
this call really is taking a long time.
KEATING: Put with all the sincerity that
a fop could put it.

He can throw a punch across the
parliament, but the bloke he should be
throwing the punch to is Howard.
Of course, he doesn't have the ticker
for it.

"I'll huff and puff and blow your house
in": that's Costello.

HE IS ALL TIP AND NO ICEBERG.
[ON PETER COSTELLO]

The greatest L-plater of all time.

This bloke Costello got hit in the arse by a rainbow. He's just got to wake up every morning and take credit for the economic outcomes I created.

I used to refer to him as thallium, a slow-acting dope. And I think that is exactly what he is.

Costello was a policy bum of the first order who squandered eleven years of economic opportunity.

This is a low-flying person.

MALCOLM FRASER

"Son, if I had a dog with eyes as close together as that, I'd shoot it."
[quoting a Queensland farmer]

LIKE AN EASTER ISLAND STATUE WITH AN ARSE FULL OF RAZOR BLADES.
[ON M ALCOLM F RASER]

The most untrustworthy prime minister in the history of Federation.

Malcolm Fraser is the most maligned person in the Liberal Party's history. There has been more rewriting of the history of Malcolm Fraser's role by the former Treasurer [John Howard] than anyone could imagine. The truth of the matter is that he could not get a piece of toilet paper or a piece of tissue paper through the Cabinet.

We see virtues in Malcolm these days we couldn't see then. But mind you, given the current [Howard] government, that is not hard to do. Just being a democrat is enough.

JOHN HEWSON

Ideologically hamstrung, ideologically divisive, politically barren ... a cold fish washed ashore by the recession; a primitive species we haven't seen before in this country.

He's returning to Fightback! Like Wile E. Coyote, he's returning to the scene of the accident. He said "the essential philosophy of Fightback! has to be preserved" – like the coyote waiting for the anvil to drop from the sky.

An abacus gone feral.

A dog with a belly full of piss.

I have a psychological hold over Hewson ... He's like a stone statue in the cemetery.

I'm not going to be fairy-flossed away as my opposite number, John Hewson, is prepared to be flossed away by some spaced-out, vacuous ad agency.

Dr Hewson often says he comes from a suburb not far from mine. But I say, so what? At least I'm still representing my people. What connection do you have with them now you're representing the blue-rinse set from Vaucluse and the real estate agents from Mosman?

We have just had a motion moved by the Shadow Treasurer, the Honourable Member for Wentworth, who could not sustain the debate. It was the limpest performance I have ever seen. Seven minutes into the speech he could not sustain it. It was like being flogged with a warm lettuce. It was like being mauled by a dead sheep.

The Leader of the Opposition always turns around when I drop one on him. He cannot psychologically handle it.

If the honourable member wishes to behave like a ninny, he cannot complain.

This little flower, this delicate little beauty, this cream puff, is supposed to be beyond personal criticism...

KEATING [TO HEWSON]: You fraud. You disgraceful, disgusting fraud.
WAL FIFE: I ask the Deputy Prime Minister to withdraw those remarks.
KEATING: Of course I will not withdraw them.
"Disgusting" is not unparliamentary, you clown.

This is the sort of little-boy, stamp-yourfoot stuff which comes from a financial market yuppie who has been shoehorned into parliament.

I was implying that the Honourable Member for Wentworth was like a lizard on a rock: alive, but looking dead.

Whenever you put your hand in your pocket, Dr Hewson's hand will be there, too.
[on Hewson's GST proposal]

*HE WAS SIMPLY LIKE A SHIVER
LOOKING FOR A SPINE TO RUN UP.*
[ON JOHN HEWSON]

HEWSON: I ask the Prime Minister: if you are so confident about your view of Fightback!, why will you not call an early election?

KEATING: The answer is, mate, because I want to do you slowly. There has to be a bit of sport in this for all of us. In the psychological battle stakes, we are stripped down and ready to go. I want to see those ashen-faced performances. I want more of them. I want to be encouraged. I want to see you squirm out of this load of rubbish over a number of months. There will be no easy execution for you. You have perpetrated one of the great mischiefs on the Australian public with this thing [Fightback!], trying to rip away our social wage, trying to rip away the Australian values which we built up in our society over a century.

[Hewson] doesn't seem to carry all that personal venom that some of his colleagues carry. I give him marks for that.

BOB HAWKE

Pull out, digger. The dogs are pissing on your swag. [allegedly to Hawke, after he refused to vacate the Prime Ministership]

Old Jellyback.

Old Silver.

The trouble is we are dealing with a sports junkie here [Hawke]. I go out for a piss and they pull this one on me. Well, that's the last time I leave you two alone. From now on I'm sticking to you two like shit to a blanket. [allegedly to John Brown, Minister for Sport, who was proposing a 110% tax deduction for contributors to a Sports Foundation]

I say to him [Hawke] something that always gets him to bite: "I'm on a unity ticket with Patrick White. I think sport has the potential to addle the Australian consciousness." He bites every time.

In the end I'd execute him.

ANDREW PEACOCK

All feathers and no meat.

They were not for the show pony.
[on the US impression of Peacock]

He wanted to get back in the 747 to
hightail it to Washington into the
cocktail party circuits – that is, when
he was not standing at the mirror
running a little dye through his hair.

It is the first time the honourable
gentleman has got out from under the
sunlamp.

You have been into the dye pot again,
Andrew.

He is a part of the bunyip aristocracy,
a remnant of the failed upper class, one
of the crowd who reside in Melbourne
and govern Australia while the rest of
us are supposed to pay the penalty.

DOES A SOUFFLE RISE TWICE?
[ON ANDREW PEACOCK]

The address by the Leader of the Opposition was made with all the sincerity of a Mississippi gambler. What a squalid opportunist he is.

We are not interested in the views of painted, perfumed gigolos.

Bib and Bub: the Leader of the Opposition and his deputy...

KEATING: Mr Speaker, if this gutless spiv, and I refer to him as a gutless spiv—
SPEAKER: Order! The Treasurer will resume his seat.

What we have here is an intellectual rust bucket. The bucket might be painted up, but there is rust underneath the duco.

I suppose that the honourable gentleman's hair, like his intellect, will recede into the darkness.

He represents nothing and nobody.

WINNING CARRIES RESPONSIBILITY, AND HE SHIES OFF RESPONSIBILITY LIKE DRACULA FROM A WOODEN STAKE.
[ON ANDREW PEACOCK]

The Leader of the Opposition is more to be pitied than despised, the poor old thing.
The Liberal Party ought to put him down like a faithful old dog because he is no use to it and of no use to the nation.

JOHN HOWARD

He has more hide than a team of elephants.

...the worst thing that's come our way in Australian public life in a long, long time.

He would do a deal with the devil to become leader of the Liberal Party because little Johnny Howard must succeed.

When you say to people, "You can't get together at work, you can't organise your conditions," you're back to the earlier part of the Industrial Revolution.
And that's where Howard belongs.
He's a pre-Copernican obscurantist.

IT'S JUST HOWARD BEING HOWARD, ISN'T IT, YOU KNOW. THE LITTLE DESSICATED COCONUT IS UNDER PRESSURE AND HE IS ATTACKING ANYTHING HE CAN GET HIS HANDS ON.

[ON JOHN HOWARD]

Twice a day on radio, the guy did no thinking.
When a country has a leader that does not think, then that country starts to move back.

I go around every day pretending I'm me.
John Howard goes around every day pretending he's someone else.

I've never understood why the John Howards and the Geoffrey Blaineys et al. are defensive, so resistant to novelty and to progress. They are more than conservatives. They are reactionaries. Whatever the Leader of the Opposition may think of me, I will be around long enough to see him rolled in the political dustbin.

I'm going to put an axe right in his chest and rip his ribs apart.
We've used the levers to pull Australia into a slowdown. We will use the levers to pull it out. But when Mr Howard and his former economics adviser

Dr Hewson had the levers, it was like a Laurel and Hardy film: when they went for the handbrake it came off in their hands.

For John Howard to get to any high moral ground he would have to first climb out of the volcanic hole he's dug for himself over the last decade. You know, it's like one of those deep diamond mine holes in South Africa, you know, they're about a mile underground. He'd have to come a mile up to get to even equilibrium, let alone have any contest in morality with Kevin Rudd.

Can you imagine the cynicism and the deceptiveness of this person? He absolutely stays away from the truth like Dracula from a wooden stake. If he has a choice between telling the truth or telling a downright lie, he will take the lie every time.

WHAT WE HAVE GOT HERE IS A DEAD CARCASS, SWINGING IN THE BREEZE, BUT NOBODY WILL CUT IT DOWN TO REPLACE HIM.
[ON HOWARD'S GRIP ON THE LIBERAL LEADERSHIP IN 1988]

The old coconut's still sitting there,
Araldited to the seat.

The Honourable Member for Bennelong
is so gutless he runs away from a
debate with me.
When he gets a bit of guts back he
should take me on and I will make a
mess of him.

From this day onwards, Mr Howard will
wear his leadership like a crown of
thorns and in the parliament I will do
everything I can to crucify him.
[after Wilson Tuckey referred to
Keating's ex-fianceé in Parliament]

He is the classic non-deliverer of
Australian politics. He is the one person
who just cannot cut the mustard. The
game is too hard for him. Lurking in
his chest is not a heart for the political
fight, but a split pea.

He is the greatest job and investment
destroyer since the bubonic plague.

JOHN HOWARD ALWAYS POPS UP AT THESE OCCASIONS – HE'S AT EVERY NATIONAL, INTERNATIONAL CATASTROPHE, SORT OF REPRESENTATIVE OF WHITE LADY FUNERALS.

I will never get to the stage of wanting to lead the nation standing in front of the mirror each morning clipping the eyebrows here and clipping the eyebrows there with Janette and the kids: it is like spot the eyebrows.

What possible use could a modern Australia – a country joining its region for the first time in its history, becoming an outward-looking country, getting low inflation and high productivity – have for a man who describes himself as the most conservative leader the Liberal Party has ever had? What use do you think you are to indigenous Australia? What use do you think you are to Asia, to our immigration?

Howard certainly shifted our moral compass. He has bruised our soul. He has played to the basest of human instincts. He has, with his wages policy alone, turned our sense of fairness and egalitarianism on its head. He has sinned mightily.

I AM NOT LIKE THE LEADER OF THE OPPOSITION. I DID NOT SLITHER OUT OF THE CABINET ROOM LIKE A MANGY MAGGOT.
[ON JOHN HOWARD]

Then, of course, we have this sort of morbid rhetoric – the sort of small, thrifty shopkeeper gnarlishness with the red tape of government spending. We have all this anti-government spending rhetoric, but in his day he was the big spender – Mr 28.8% of GDP. Look, John, do not waste your time on me, son. I have been around. I know you. I know where the skeletons are in your closet.

I did a little ditty in here about a family walking through a museum. They are looking around and the kid says, "Mum, what's that?" She says, "Well, son, that is the Morphy Richards toaster. We used to have one. We used to put the bread in that. You had to wind it down and turn it on." The kid says, "What's this?" She says, "That is the Qualcast mower. We had one of those at home." He says, "Who is this?" She says, "That's John Howard. He was the Treasurer who put Australia into moribund low growth back in the 1970s and the 1980s." The boy says, "But what is he, Mum?" She says, "He is the future, son."

WILSON TUCKEY

KEATING: The Deputy Leader of the Opposition, after we have clocked up these phenomenal growth rates, says: "You had the growth numbers wrong. You had the outlay numbers wrong." We did not have them wrong. We had them dead right, and we have them right again.

WILSON TUCKEY: All you have done is finance growth with debt.

KEATING: You boxhead, you would not know. You are flat out counting past ten.

TUCKEY: Mr Deputy Speaker, I take a point of order. I ask for that remark to be withdrawn.

KEATING: I will withdraw it if you shut up for a while.

TUCKEY: I will shut up in the normal way I have to. You are an idiot. You are just a hopeless nong. You would not know.

KEATING: Shut up! Sit down and shut up, you pig!

YOU STUPID, FOUL-MOUTHED GRUB.
[ON WILSON TUCKEY]

KEATING: Mr Deputy Speaker, the Honourable Member for O'Connor is a member with a criminal intellect, and is a criminal in my view.

TUCKEY: Withdraw.

DEPUTY SPEAKER: The Honourable Member for O'Connor has claimed that the words used by the Treasurer were offensive to him. Will the Treasurer withdraw?

KEATING: I will withdraw nothing.

TUCKEY: I have now ... been accused of having a criminal intellect, and I ask that that be withdrawn. I certainly do not mix with criminals.

KEATING: I do not get someone to hold somebody against a wall while I belt him with a truncheon.

You piece of criminal garbage.
[after Tuckey implied a child had been involved in Keating's 1973 break-up with his fiancée]

As a dog returns to its vomit, so a fool repeats his folly.
[after Tuckey again mentioned Keating's ex-fiancée]

Mr Deputy Speaker, this clown continues to interject in perpetuity.

The honourable member is a half-baked crim.

The loopy crim from O'Connor is at it again.

IAN SINCLAIR

This piece of vermin, the Leader of the National Party...

Let the Leader of the National Party go to the Supreme Court, and let us see how some of the glib rubbish, tripe and drivel he went on with last week goes before a Supreme Court justice in a defamation proceeding.

The Right Honourable Member for New England has demonstrated at last that there is no limit to how far he will stoop, no gutter too low to slide into, no sewer too murky for him to lose himself in.

WHAT WE HAVE AS A LEADER OF THE NATIONAL PARTY IS A POLITICAL CARCASS WITH A COAT AND TIE ON.
[ON IAN SINCLAIR]

JIM CARLTON

I was nearly chloroformed by the performance of the Honourable Member for Mackellar. It nearly put me right out for the afternoon.

JIM CARLTON: Mr Deputy Speaker, I raise a point of order.
KEATING: Here is old Rosie again. She is up again.

We on this side of the House do not call him Carlton Light for nothing.

MISCELLANEOUS INSULTS

He has never been thoughtful, and he has never been a thinker. What we have here is just bigotry. It is the voice of ignorance, the voice of hysteria and the voice of the nineteenth century.
[on Hugh Morgan]

HE COULD NOT RAFFLE A DUCK IN A PUB.
[ON JIM CARLTON]

...get going in a barrel of yeast.
[what most Australian businesspeople
could not do]

I will be ripping [NSW Liberal Rosemary
Foot] into shreds in the courts at the
right moment. She can go and shoot
her big mouth off in the Supreme
Court. We will see how she goes there.

I do not mind getting up here every
day to respond to these inane
propositions, but it is hardly worth the
effort to reply to the sort of drivel that
has been put to me.

The Deputy Prime Minister, who is the
gigolo for any foreign interest which
wants to come to this country, has no
semblance whatsoever of the national
interest...
[on Doug Anthony]

Look at [Nick] Greiner.
He's only two years old and already
he's terminal.

I HAVEN'T GOT MUCH TIME FOR WIMPS, AND THERE ARE A LOT OF WIMPS AROUND.

The brain-damaged Honourable Member for Bruce made his first parliamentary contribution since being elected by calling a quorum to silence me for three minutes.
[on Ken Aldred]

Do not worry about him, Mr Deputy Speaker. He has got the political morals of an alley cat.
[on Michael Hodgman]

Mate, he's brain-dead. What can you do with a poor silly bastard like that? I spent 90 minutes on the phone with him – 90 fucking minutes – and I barely got him to add up two plus two.
[on Michael Hatton]

The honourable member has been in so many parties he is a complete political harlot.
[on Steele Hall]

Harlots, sleazebags, frauds, immoral, cheats, blackguards, pigs, mugs, clowns, boxheads, criminal intellects, criminals, stupid crooks, corporate crooks, friends of tax cheats, brain-damaged, loopy crims, stupid foul-mouthed grub, piece of criminal garbage, dullards, stupid, mindless, crazy, alley cat, bunyip aristocracy, clot, fop, gigolo, hare-brained, hillbilly, malcontent, mealy-mouthed, ninny, rustbucket, scumbag, scum, sucker, thug, dimwits, dummies, a swill, a pig sty, Liberal muck, vile constituency, fools and incompetents, rip-off merchants, perfumed gigolos, gutless spiv, glib rubbish, tripe and drivel, constitutional vandals, stunned mullets, half-baked crim, insane stupidities, champion liar, ghouls of the National Party, barnyard bullies, piece of parliamentary filth. [Keating invective in Parliament, as compiled by Mungo MacCallum]

HE'S A BIG BAD BASTARD AND THE ONLY WAY YOU CAN DEAL WITH HIM IS TO MAKE SURE HE THINKS YOU CAN BE A BIG BAD BASTARD TOO.
[ON RUPERT MURDOCH]

That you, Jim [McClelland]? Paul Keating here. Just because you swallowed a fucking dictionary when you were about fifteen doesn't give you the right to pour a bucket of shit over the rest of us.

[Mike] Codd will be lucky to get a job cleaning shithouses if I ever become prime minister.

LABOR

We are the reform party in this country.

You need me more than I need you. [to Whitlam, after he requested Keating's vote in caucus]

It really surprises me that some people in this party think we owe Westpac something. Or the ANZ Bank. Or the National.

GOUGH WHITLAM: THAT WAS A GOOD SPEECH. YOU SHOULD GO BACK, COMRADE, AND GET YOURSELF AN HONOURS DEGREE.
KEATING: WHAT FOR?
THEN I'D BE LIKE YOU.

Of the Whitlam generation, Whitlam was the only good one. Of the Hawke generation, only Hawke could win. Of my generation, now that I've gone, there's nothing left. They haven't done much, have they, Beazley, Crean, Evans, Lawrence, all the ones in their fifties?

[Brian] Burke is smarter than two-thirds of the Western Australian Labor Party rolled together. That's why he keeps bobbing up.

The romantics who choose to regard the 1972 Whitlam program as a purist application of high-minded Labor principle ... The truth is the program was essentially about winning votes.

Whitlam's greatest achievement in the late 1960s was to take the party by the scruff of its neck and drag it towards the contemporary reality and the real influence of the workforce. He made Labor relevant again.

The Labor Cabinet from 1972 to 1975 had no overarching philosophy. Certainly no economic one. And the meetings, of course, were mayhem. Twenty-seven ministers all having their say. Much of it entirely undisciplined. As one of the few people who sat through the Cabinets of those years and of the later years in the 1980s and 1990s, the difference could not have been starker. It was like comparing a well-meaning but ambitious group on a municipal finance committee with the people running the re-purchasing operations of the Bank of England.

In terms of the Labor agenda, this [Hawke] government has left every other Labor government before it bare-arsed. No other Labor government even gets within cooee of it. We have a Cabinet which has a degree of economic sophistication which puts the Whitlam government into the caveman class.

Fundamentally, the Labor Party never believed in the model. The Labor Party never believed in the model that Hawke and I gave the country, but it happened. The country got a very great break from it.

They'll do him no good. Because in the end, those kind of conservative tea-leaf-reading focus-group-driven polling types who I think led Kim [Beazley] into nothingness – he's got his life to repent in leisure now at what they did to him – they're back. They're back. Gary Gray lost the '96 election with me and then lost '98. He's been given Kim Beazley's best seat in Western Australia. The Labor Party is not going to profit from having these proven unsuccessful people around who are frightened of their own shadow and won't get out of bed in the morning unless they've had a focus group report to tell them which side of bed to get out.

Kim [Beazley] today gave us the quote from Lenin about Labor parties being bourgeois. He should wear that quote like a badge of honour; that our creed survived and his didn't. Because we did represent, and always have represented, the working class.

When I grew up about 30% of the community were Catholics but about 50 to 60% of the working class were Catholics. So, there was never any way we were going to be Marxist–Leninist.

We were and are a pluralist party; we've given a home to all sorts of people – Fabians, Marxists, single-taxers; all sorts of characters.

This is the sweetest victory of all. This is a victory for the true believers; the people who, in difficult times, have kept the faith.

[After winning the 1993 federal election]

HIMSELF

If someone puts you on a pedestal – and the big pedestal-builder first was my grandmother – something sticks with you all your life. You've got to go through life with someone thinking you're special. You know, when you've got to get the sword out for real combat, I think having the sort of love quotient working for you is very powerful.

We don't want to be sparkling and happy all the time. You need the inner life, the inner sadness. It is what fills you out.

KERRY O'BRIEN: Why were you interested in learning about power at eighteen?
KEATING: That's the business I had decided I wanted to be in.

Having enemies worries some people; for me, it is a badge of honour.

POLITICIANS COME IN THREE VARIETIES: STRAIGHT MEN, FIXERS AND MADDIES.

Would I write a better book?
Well, of course I would.
I write better than George [Megalogenis]
and I know more.
[launching Megalogenis's *The Longest Decade*]

The Placido Domingo of Australian politics.

THE LIBERALS & THE COALITION

A party of primitives, throw-backs to nineteenth-century robber-baron capitalism, those who believe that what we should do is make way for the wealthy because in their slipstream the rest will pick up something on the way through.
The hollow men of the Liberal Party...

Some of you are old enough to remember cracker night, I'm sure. I sometimes think of my opponents sitting on the front bench as crackers, with Hewson the skyrocket. And Howard, always with such promise. He always reminded me of that thing called the flower pot. Now, I don't know if any of you remember the flower pot, but that was the one which always promised a dazzling performance. You'd light it up, and it had multicolours, and it did a show for you but, often, when you lit it up it went fffftt, you know, a bit of a spark ... there was always a bit of a show, and then there'd be a bit more, and a bit more, then, finally, it fell away to nothing. Then there's [Ian] McLachlan, our establishment friend, who was supposed to have come to Canberra with a big bang. I always think of him as the bunger, you know, the big red bungers ... the strong, silent type capable of a big bang. You light it up, everyone stands back, and then the wick goes down ... and everyone's waiting ... and they keep on waiting ... and that's it, it doesn't go off. And then there's Bronwyn [Bishop]. She reminds me of the Catherine wheel. We used to nail them to the fence and they'd take off, spreadeagle the kids, burn the dog, run up a tree and then fizzle out going round in circles. So, that's our friends in the Opposition. Bitter, burnt out and accident-prone.

This was the country that you people wedded yourself to, and even as it walked out on you and joined the Common Market, you were still looking for your MBEs and your knighthoods and the rest of the regalia that comes with it. [on the Coalition's affinity with Britain]

You know sometimes when you see people at factories, they've been in a plant that's got toxic stuff, they get hosed down? I felt on Saturday night I'd been hosed down.
[after the Coalition's 2007 loss]

This is the kind of question you get from the lice.
[House of Representatives, in response to a question from David Connolly]

VOTES FOR COALITION MEMBERS WHO HAVE ALWAYS BEEN CHEATS, CHEATS, CHEATS AND WILL ALWAYS BE CHEATS, CHEATS, CHEATS.

This intellectual rabble.

You ought to be ashamed of yourselves. Is it any wonder the country has written you off? Is it any wonder you are held in universal contempt by all thinking people around the country?

Small-time punk stuff coming from a punk Opposition. The public of Australia can make the appropriate judgement when we squash the parliamentary garbage opposite at the next poll.

The cowards of the National Party, the hillbillies of the National Party, have only ever stood for sticking their hands in the public purse and handing it to a small constituency. The whole reason for their existence in politics is putrid. It is absolutely putrid to think that they have legitimised themselves since the 1920s when their leader climbed the back stairs and did the dirty deal with Stanley Melbourne Bruce. Earl Page did the dirty deal and from that day on that vile constituency, the National Party, did nothing else but get its hand in the public purse.

If one travels around the rest of the world – does the rounds of Wall Street, the City of London, and Frankfurt, to see what they think of honourable members opposite – one finds that they think honourable members opposite are a joke and that they have no economic respectability left. They are regarded as a party of fools, which is what they are.

Madam Deputy Speaker, take no notice of the Liberals on tax. They are rip-off merchants.

The issue here is whether we would see under Hewson one of the most spiteful, vile governments in the Western world.

THE GALL OF YOU!
THE VICIOUSNESS OF YOU!

We have given Australia back its future. As a trading country it can lift its head up around the world. What are we left with? The dullards of the Opposition who did not know what to do.

These vicious, unprincipled people, from the Leader of the Opposition down, employ the most personalised remarks, the most specific personal charges against ministers in this parliament, as no Opposition has ever done before.

The Liberals aren't a real political party. They're an outfit. They can only define themselves by saying they're anti-Labor.

The fact is that they are the thugs of Australian politics. They are the constitutional vandals of Australia. They are greedy for power. They would rip up the Constitution, attack any convention or any individual to get their own way.

MR SPEAKER, CAN I HAVE SOME PROTECTION FROM THE CLOWNS ON THE FRONT BENCH?

THOSE OPPOSITE COULD NOT OPERATE A TART SHOP.

They still believe they're the
born-to-rule squad.

They are a bunch of nobodies going
nowhere.

I'll spend my time climbing over the
Liberals. Think how weak they are.

We will see a repeat of what we saw
in 1988, which was basically about how
we shouldn't have more Asians here,
we shouldn't have Asians in this
country. I mean, if you scratch most of
these characters, what you get is a little
bit of that sort of talk.

Conservative governments are at least
supposed to believe in thrift. God
knows, they don't believe in much else.

There is something odd about Australian
conservatives. It is that, in some
important ways, they aren't
conservatives at all. Whatever else you
say about conservative political
philosophies, you can usually rely upon
their followers to cherish institutions of
state ... Out here, though, we've ended

up with conservatives who treat the institutions of state with contempt. From the High Court to the Australian Public Service to the Australian Defence Force to the nature of the governor-generalship, the Howard government has been damaging those institutions rather than preserving them. Undermining them, not defending them.

These people say they believe in the rule of law, except the laws they do not like.

INTERNATIONAL RELATIONS

I learned [at school] about self-respect and self-regard for Australia – not about some cultural cringe to a country which decided not to defend the Malaysian Peninsula, not to worry about Singapore, and not to give our troops back [from fighting in the Middle East] to keep ourselves free from Japanese domination.

YOU ARE A SKUNK AT A PICNIC.
[TO AL GORE AT AN APEC LEADERS' MEETING]

The [Howard] government's problems with foreign policy stem from its own insecurity; from a defensive and uncertain view of Australia and its place in the world. A sense that we should know our place, that we shouldn't get ideas above our station. A government that has little faith in Australians or what they are capable of.

Of course, I liked the Queen, and let me tell you, I think she liked me. She sat me next to her on the *Britannia,* among other places. When things got a little boring, she and I would have a competition as to who made the silver on the table. At one point she said to her private secretary, "I think the Prime Minister's trying to get away with my silver."

Europe is just ossified compared to this place.

Why muck around with the Dutch and the Swedes in the G10?
It's a mushroom club anyway.

APEC is bigger than all of us –
Australia, the US and Malaysia, and Dr
Mahathir and any other recalcitrants.

Don't ask me any more questions about
Mahathir. I couldn't care less, frankly,
whether he comes [to APEC] or not
next year.

The region's undisputed elder statesman.
[on President Suharto of Indonesia]

More than any figure in the post-Second
World War period, including any
American president, President Suharto,
by his judgement, goodwill and good
sense, had the greatest positive impact
on Australia's strategic environment and,
hence, its history.

Why have Australians regarded
Indonesia so suspiciously, especially over
the last quarter-century, when it is
evident that Indonesia has been the
fulcrum of our strategic stability?
Unfortunately, I think the answer is
Timor and the wilful reporting of
Indonesian affairs in Australia by the
Australian press...

Anyone in the political game worldwide knew Iraq was a decimated country after the sanctions and the war in 1991. There was no way that they were building weapons of mass destruction, much less having the ability to deliver them, and certainly not nuclear weapons. I would never have committed troops to Iraq in those circumstances – ever.

Iraq is a country in civil war. John Howard committed Australian troops to that conflagration and history will bring him to account for it.

ELEANOR HALL: Should Kevin Rudd have been clever enough to try and avoid contact with Brian Burke, knowing his reputation?
KEATING: Look, look, Kevin has done something, he's met Brian Burke.

IN THE END IT'S THE BIG PICTURE WHICH CHANGES NATIONS, AND WHATEVER OUR OPPONENTS MAY SAY, AUSTRALIA'S CHANGED INEXORABLY FOR GOOD, FOR THE BETTER.

But I'll tell you what he hasn't done. He hasn't lied to his nation about reasons for committing Australia to a non-UN sponsored invasion and war. He hasn't turned his head from the plight of a boat full of wretched individuals looking for shelter, and then adding insult to injury by saying they threw their kids overboard first, you know. And he hasn't prostituted the UN Oil-for-Food program by falsely declaring that Australia's wheat shipments were not *ultra vires* of the UN guidelines.

I think the rise of China is one of the great events of all economic and human history, and I think this will be overwhelmingly a positive thing for the region and the world.

We fought two world wars over the status of Germany. Two. We don't want to be fighting one over China.

ECONOMICS

If this Government cannot get the adjustment, get manufacturing going again, and keep moderate wage outcomes and a sensible economic policy, then Australia is basically done for. We will end up being a third-rate economy ... a banana republic.

The accounts do show that Australia is in a recession. The most important thing about that is, is that this is the recession that Australia had to have.

Australia feels better, because it is better. Indeed, since September 1991, Australia's economy began its now continuous thirteen-year stretch of growth ... And I am sure you will give me the latitude to say that none of this had anything to do with John Howard or Peter Costello. Apart from the Howard government's GST, no other important structural change has been put into place. And I do not regard a GST, a tax change, as having important structural influences. A GST does not change economic behaviour, it simply collects revenue. Howard and Costello have simply traded off the structural benefits bequeathed to them by my government. They have made hay while the sun has shone, providing buckets of revenue to the annual budgets in measures that they could hardly believe.

PETER LEWIS: What would you say to the blue-collar workers who have seen their jobs lost in Australia?
KEATING: What is your new job like? One of the 2.5 million created since the early 1980s. People have found better jobs. I mean, did we ever hurt anybody liberating them from the car assembly line? When they left the car assembly line and got a more interesting job in the economy, did we do them a disservice? Of course we didn't. And the way people talk about this free and fair trade as if the economy is static and not dynamic, and a job lost is not a job replaced, is just bunkum ... some of these people like [Doug] Cameron et al. think we can ... insulate ourselves, while at the same time having a growing standard of living – it's tripe.

THE BIG PICTURE

No choice we can make as a nation lies between our history and our geography. We can hardly change either of them. They are immutable. The only choice we can make as a nation is the choice about our future.

All countries need a break in their history. The great break for us was the post-war migration program. It made us more diverse, more interesting, more vibrant and gave us more critical mass.

You know, when we put our Federation together, there were no Washingtons around, no soldier-statesmen, no people like Jefferson talking about blood being the fertiliser of democracy. Our Federation was put together by lawyers and businessmen – mostly old forelock-tuggers – people who set us up as a British satellite. They were little nationalists. Safe little nationalists.

It begins, I think, with that act of recognition. Recognition that it was we who did the dispossessing. We took the traditional lands and smashed the traditional way of life. We brought the diseases. The alcohol. We committed the murders. We took the children from their mothers. We practised discrimination and exclusion. It was our ignorance and our prejudice. And our failure to imagine these things being done to us. With some noble exceptions, we failed to make the most basic human response and enter into their hearts and minds. We failed to ask – how would I feel if this were done to me?

WHEN ONE HAS BEEN TOUCHED BY THE STELLAR POWER AND ETHEREAL PLAYING OF A SUBLIME MUSICIAN, ONE IS LIFTED, IF ONLY BRIEFLY, TO A PLACE BEYOND THE REALM OF THE TEMPORAL.

You just can't have a position where some pumped-up bunyip potentate dismisses an elected government.

My own views on the Republic are unchanged and utterly unshaken. Our head of state has to be one of us.

When the government changes, the country changes.

The dogs may bark but the caravan moves on.

Back Cover Material

Presenting the one and only Paul Keating – at his straight-shooting, scumbag-calling, merciless best.

Paul lets rip – on John Howard: "The little desiccated coconut is under pressure and he is attacking anything he can get his hands on."

On Peter Costello: "The thing about poor old Costello is he is all tip and no iceberg."

On John Hewson: [His performance is] like being flogged with a warm lettuce."

On Andrew Peacock: "What we have here is an intellectual rust bucket."

On Wilson Tuckey: "You stupid, foul-mouthed grub."

On Tony Abbott: "If Tony Abbott ends up the prime minister of Australia, you've got to say, God help us."

And that's just a taste...

RUSSELL MARKS is the online editor at the *Monthly* and an honorary associate at La Trobe University. He has worked as a criminal defence lawyer and an academic. He compiled *Tony Speaks! The Wisdom of the Abbott* (revised edition 2014), *Kattertonia: The Wit and Wisdom of Bob Katter* (2013), and is currently writing a book on the criminal justice system.